Hello?
Can You Hear Me?

HOW TO CREATE HARMONY WITH YOUR ANIMAL COMPANIONS BY TUNING INTO ANIMAL LANGUAGE

A BOOK BY

BIANCA DE REUS

BALBOA.
PRESS
A DIVISION OF HAY HOUSE

Balboa Press books may be ordered through
booksellers or by contacting:

Balboa Press
A Division of Hay House
1663 Liberty Drive
Bloomington, IN 47403
www.balboapress.com.au
1 (877) 407-4847

Because of the dynamic nature of the Internet, any web addresses or
links contained in this book may have changed since publication and
may no longer be valid. The views expressed in this work are solely those
of the author and do not necessarily reflect the views of the publisher,
and the publisher hereby disclaims any responsibility for them.

The author of this book does not dispense medical advice or prescribe
the use of any technique as a form of treatment for physical,
emotional, or medical problems without the advice of a physician,
either directly or indirectly. The intent of the author is only to offer
information of a general nature to help you in your quest for emotional
and spiritual well-being. In the event you use any of the information
in this book for yourself, which is your constitutional right, the author
and the publisher assume no responsibility for your actions.

Print information available on the last page.

ISBN: 978-1-5043-1494-7 (sc)
ISBN: 978-1-5043-1495-4 (e)

Balboa Press rev. date: 10/16/2018

I believe every animal has a story to
tell and knowledge to share with
the world.
It is the people who are open to
listening to the animal kingdom and
receiving these stories and
knowledge who will help the animal
kingdom share their stories and
knowledge with us humans,
so we can learn,
be inspired and create a
positive change in ourselves and
in the world.

Dedication

I dedicate this book to my wife and soulmate, Lana, to our son Michael and our two beautiful mini Schnauzers, Rosie & Toby.

Without you this book would not be a reality.

THANK YOU so much for your unconditional love and support during the writing of this book; it truly has been a 5-year brian!

I love you so much!
♡

I also dedicate this book to all Soul Beings on this beautiful planet and in the Universe: Mother Earth (Gaia), the animal kingdom, the plant kingdom, and fellow humans.

May we serve each other well and look after ourselves and each other.

May we all listen to each other's wisdom, stories, and knowledge, learn from each other, and together create a wonderful, happy and healthy environment for all of us to live together, in connectedness, unconditional love and light.

Contents

Foreword

Clare Mann

Psychologist, Communications Trainer and Author
www.veganpsychologist.com

Over the years clients have shared stories of experiences about loved ones who have died. These sometimes include sightings or, more commonly, a sense of the other being's presence.

I have had such experiences, and the most poignant occurred after my mother died. I recall on the day of her funeral looking out of the window of her bedroom at a large oak tree. We had shared this view over the decades and on that day, caught in the grip of searing grief, I was aware that she had gone. Only moments before, I had gone through her clothes hanging in the wardrobe, holding them to my face, desperate to capture one more time her smell and warmth.

As I stood looking out of that window, I experienced something that changed my life forever. As I looked out, she was looking out at the exact same time, through my eyes, our eyes. I experienced the sensation of her simultaneously looking at me and me looking at her. We were not separate and nor was the oak tree. Words do little justice to this experience which was truly existential in nature. In that moment, I experienced non-separation and felt I had grasped something of the nature of what this journey is all about.

In the last seven years, I have lost two canine companions: Topaz, who was seventeen and Dasien, who was fifteen. The loss of one's canine children is one of the deepest losses I have ever felt, but that experience some fifteen years earlier with my mother reminds me that life and death are inextricably linked, and death is not the end.

When people talk about communicating with animals, their experiences are quickly dismissed as being anthropomorphic and sentimental, yet anyone who has ever had the honour of sharing an animal's life, knows that such communication is not only real but teaches us something that perhaps we have forgotten.

In our modern world, with science as the arbiter of all truth, we are encouraged to dismiss that which we can't prove, and animal communication is one of those. Thank goodness for people like Bianca de Reus, who pays scant attention to such naysayers, instead building on the gift she has been given to communicate with all animals.

In this book, Bianca has shown us that far from being sentimental or irrational, communicating with animals is something that we can all do. Her book offers a fresh approach to not only understanding the animals we live with but invites us to expand our bandwidth of compassion to other animals beyond our companions.

All animals, whether they be wildlife, farmed animals, or those imprisoned in laboratories, deserve to live their lives free from harm and for their own sakes. I believe as we learn to communicate more with our companions, we are invited to listen carefully to all animals and ensure our lifestyle choices do everything to not harm or exploit animals in any way. I believe it is only then that we will experience non-separation on this earth and feel at last that we are at home.

Amanda Powers

Founder of LeadAstray, Dog Walker and the best dressed Animal Communicator in Australia
www.leadastraymelbourne.com

They say timing is everything. I truly believe when you are ready, the right people and opportunities present themselves. Maybe this book is your opportunity – I know that meeting Bianca de Reus and doing her online course was mine!

I have always spoken to animals, the way I speak to people. I knew they understood me, but until I met Bianca, I never really heard them.

You have picked up this book for a reason, be ready for it to change your perspective, and maybe even your life's direction.

I never imagined myself as a modern-day Dr Doolittle, but here I am chatting to dogs and cats, horses and birds, and embarking on a whole new career path I never could have dreamed possible, and I couldn't be happier.

Meeting Bianca honestly changed my life. Her guidance, knowledge, and endless encouragement was exactly what I had been searching for, I just hadn't found the right teacher.

This book is an easy step by step, practical guide on how to open up and trust what you receive.

It is an enlightening and honest approach toward the gift of animal communication, a gift we all possess, but very few of us actually use.

Bianca selflessly provided me with so many valuable tools, they have changed everything for me. I am so grateful to have met her.

I wish her all the success in the world with this, her first book, and I wish you all the joy I currently feel, knowing that you too will be where I am now, in a world filled with unimaginable beauty heard by the heart.

Hello, can you hear me?

Listen, and you will...

Introduction

Have you ever wondered what goes on behind the beautiful eyes of animals? What they must be thinking, and how they experience life?

I know that every animal has a story to tell, wanting to express how they feel, and share their wisdom with the world.

How do we know they can do this, and how can we hear them?

Luckily, many people are open to listening to animals and receiving the stories, knowledge, and wisdom that helps us humans, so we can learn, be inspired, and create a positive change in ourselves and in the world.

When I am out and about in nature and around animals, they often just start talking to me. It doesn't matter whether I'm wandering amongst them or I see a picture in front of me; animals' need to communicate with me is ever present.

Whether they have a specific message or just want a chat, I find that communicating with our animal friends is a fun, healing, loving, and therapeutic experience.

Over the years, I have learned that many people are curious about what their beloved animal is thinking. What goes on in their mind? Dogs, cats, guinea pigs, birds, sheep, cows, lizards; all animals can communicate with us, and we with them.

We simply need to be quiet and listen.

As I write this book I realise that I am not only writing about animals and our communication with them; I am also being guided to share information about connection with you, your-*self*.

In my mind, the second part of the word yourself; "*self*", is an abbreviation of "*Soul Eternal Love Flame*". Our souls are eternal, operating only from unconditional love in the brightest of eternal, universal lights.

Animals tap into this all the time and without any effort, as this is their natural understanding of the world. We call this "animal instinct", but really, it's a place of absolute love and perception from which they always operate.

Be inspired

The reason I am writing this book for you and all animals is that I want you to be inspired. To encourage you to tap into this beautiful way of connecting with animals. I want you to be amazed by what the animals will share with you, and to have the capacity to do the best you can for animals who need you.

I also want you to fully understand that animals are sentient, just like you and me. They are Soul Beings, living with genuine love, absolute passion, and a desire to serve the planet and all Beings on it.

My vision is to inspire people to create love, harmony, and joy around the world, so that humans and animals may live side by side with real love and respect.

My mission is to teach humans how to connect with animals by way of spiritual communication, inspired soul connection, mentoring, and energetic healing.

This work is extremely important for us humans to experience, so that we are in the best position to create love, harmony, joy and freedom around the world.

I know I cannot do this on my own. The world is a big place, with over 7 billion people[1] and too many animals to count, (but I was curious and researched this, and came to discover over 20 billion, including insects![2])

I have a desire to help you become a compassionate animal lover and communicator.

This book lets you in on my journey with animal communication. It will teach you about connecting with animals, and how you can have a better relationship with them and yourself.

My wish is that this book will be a guide and useful tool for you to better understand animal communication. My wish is that this book will be a guide and useful tool for you to better understand animal communication. When we understand all animals, big and small, scaly and furry, we extend our compassion beyond humankind.

Communicating with all animals, from companions at home to those on the farm and out in wildlife, could be the beginning of a new and peaceful world.

You'll notice I frequently refer to the "Source" and other spiritual language. The Source refers to that wonderful energy of life, sometimes also described as God, Grace, or the Universe. If you feel more comfortable with a different term, please feel free to replace it as you read.

Allow this book to provide you with knowledge, wisdom, and inspiration to be with and care for animals.

So, take a breath, and open up to the possibility that you too can talk with animals and understand them.

Let's enjoy this journey together.

Love & Light,

Bianca

Why are you keen to learn about animal communication?

What I am wanting to gain from this book and why:

_____

_____

_____

_____

_____

_____

_____

_____

_____

_____

_____

_____

_____

_____

_____

_____

_____

_____

_____

_____

_____

_____

_____

_____

_____

_____

To be or not to be spiritual...

...It wasn't a choice

My story

Let me first start by sharing how communicating with animals became part of my life, after I first discovered some of my spiritual abilities.

I'd love this to be an insight for you; assurance that you are not alone and that you *can* learn to connect with yourself and your pet, or any other animal around you.

I was born into a loving family, with inspirational parents and a cheeky, hard-working, and handsome brother.

My brother and I were raised with love and we learned to make our own choices around what we wanted to do with our lives.

Of course, every person grows up with some challenges in their families, some more than others. I am very thankful that as I now look back, I do so with very pleasant memories of my childhood. My parents, brother and I had great times together.

Religion was not a huge part of our family, although I remember being Catholic was part of my life, especially via one of my grandmothers. But my parents never pushed any religion onto me or my brother. They felt it was up to us to decide what we wanted.

I remember I chose to be baptised into Catholicism when I was twelve years old. I learned everything I could about the stories in the bible and loved them all.

It wasn't until later in life I noticed I wasn't practising the religion and only visited, and still do visit churches because of the history and beauty of the buildings.

I knew I didn't need to practice one particular religion as I learned very quickly that all religions are about connecting with *all that is* and the Source; no matter what name it has been given. To me it's all about connecting with energy, vibration and consciousness[3]. Connecting with the Universe.

And boy, did I find out very quickly what it means to be connected to Source!

Throughout my life I have always had a *knowing* and could *feel* things. I never really knew what that was or how I could do it.

People have always and continue to come to me for guidance, advice and support. They say:

"Bianca knows everything. She will make it right."
"Bianca will help you feel better."
"Bianca will be able to guide you in the right direction or help you with clarity."

"When I am around you, you always make me feel happy, at peace and light."

Up until recently I denied knowing *everything*, but on many occasions, it was made clear to me that I did know a lot! I *feel* what is right and what is wrong; I *know* which direction to go or where to guide a person.

But I never knew how, or why.

Not knowing drove me into a spin and depression for a long time. I felt alone, and felt different. Especially in my younger years, I felt I didn't belong, and that feeling lasted to well into my adult life.

I see myself as a practical, down to earth woman, who certainly doesn't tap into the "woo-woo" of life. To me, it has to be tangible and analysed. I love to find out why things happen, and because I couldn't figure out the WHY, it drove me nuts! Why did I know so much? Why did I feel what I felt and couldn't describe it? Why didn't I know where it was coming from? And WHY did it feel like such a heavy responsibility?

Then, around 2007, things started to change on a physical level. My hands and the space between my eyebrows had sensations of tingles, heat and chills. Sounds became too loud to bear. I had no idea what was going on!

My hands were the worst. They felt big, hot and then cold, and they were tingling all the time. I ended up going to specialists to have my hands tested as I was convinced I had nerve damage.

Nothing. Everything was fine. (Phew!)

The pressure in between my eyebrows continued.

The noises in my ears were amplified to the point my ears hurt!

I was afraid to talk to anyone apart from my doctor and specialists. Even my wife, Lana, didn't understand half of what I was going through – and I was too scared to tell her. What would she think?

Finally, I spoke to my mum over the phone. She listened, and then she asked me if I could lay my hands on my legs, while I was sitting down.

I did.

The minute I put my hands on my legs, palms down, I felt an instant and massive surge of energy coming through my hands and down into my legs, straight into the ground. My whole body began to heat up and tingle. Then I felt a calmness coming over me like a warm blanket – like a beautiful hug.

I knew immediately something important and magical was happening, and this had something to do with all my physical symptoms, as well as the knowing and feeling of "things". The tension between my eyebrows changed to a moving sensation of familiarity and love. I couldn't describe it, but I knew exactly what I was to do and what I was experiencing.

From that day onwards, I started to research everything to do with energy and spiritual healing. I found the right mentors and teachers. I became a Reiki and Shambala[4] Master healer and started to practice healing on friends, family, and animals.

My daily routine was healing myself, meditation, and learning more about the metaphysical world. I came across Wayne Dyer, Doreen Virtue, Louise Hay, Marianne Williamson, Esther Hicks, and Caroline Myss. All beautiful mentors and teachers from whom I learned so much about the spiritual world. My own world started to expand.

My depression, coupled with not really knowing how to apply this knowledge, was still a struggle every day. I didn't know what I needed to do with all my newfound skills and abilities, including my intuition about people around me - people I couldn't see. I learned more about this and started following John Edward[5], who, in my opinion, keeps it real and logical. He taught me that it is very normal to have this ability, and I took his learning on board and started to have fun with it. I can now happily say I am who I am, and I can do what I do, because it is part of me.

Now that I have animal communication as another layer in my abilities on this earth plane[6], I am living fully from my heart, being who I truly am.

Growing up with animals

Animals have always played a big part in my life, having grown up with dogs, horses, guinea pigs, and many others. My parents always had dogs, and later birds at home. I was always thinking about what it would be like to be able to understand what they had to say, what they were thinking, and how they were feeling.

Every year, my parents took my brother and I on holidays, and we travelled around the country or throughout Europe. One of our favourite places to go was a family holiday park approximately two hours from our home. There were horses there. I loved hanging out with them! I looked after them by feeding them, brushing their manes and simply spending time with them. It lifted me up and I always felt so energised.

To this day I still feel the same around animals. I love all animals, no matter what breed or species they are. Yes, I even learned to love spiders and snakes!

I have to admit I am biased towards horses and dogs. And cheetahs - all of my life I have loved cheetahs! They are my personal inspiration for strength, determination, and focus.

Currently we have two beautiful dogs in our family: Rosie and Toby. They are fifteen-year-old mini-Schnauzers. Rosie and Toby have been with me since they were born, and have been absolute rocks in my life. They spoil me and my family with unconditional love, support, and guidance, not to mention fun!

Before I learned animal communication, I always wondered what was going on behind their gorgeous eyes. They would sometimes stare at me as if to say; "Don't you know what we mean, mum?" Toby especially could stare at me all day!

I would apologise profusely for not being able to hear them, and then I would guess what they wanted to have or tell me. I didn't always guess the right thing though. All I knew was look at their ears, tails, and behaviour to try and understand if I was on the right path with them.

As I already worked with animals through Reiki, I do remember sometimes seeing colours and images during the healing process. But never in a million years would I have guessed the next thing would happen!

Animals are sentient beings.

Treat them with respect,
unconditional love and compassion.

Only then will you hear their voice.

Tuning in to animal language

My encounter with a snake

"Hello? Can you hear me?"

I heard the words whilst I was sitting with a dear friend on an old, fallen tree trunk, in 2011. We'd stopped for a bite to eat during our bushwalk, and I asked her if she'd said anything. She hadn't.

I thought I was hearing things, so I brushed it off and didn't pay it any attention. Then I heard it again:

"Hello? Hello? Can you hear me?" Again I ignored it but I heard it again, with a bit more force this time. I heard it up to five times, before finally, in my mind, I asked who it was. The following conversation took place:

"Great, you can finally hear me! I am here to tell you to go out into the world and do your job."

I asked, *"Who are you, and what do you mean?"*

It replied, *"I am a snake, and I am under the tree"*

"Oh okay. Wow"

The snake said, *"I am just testing to find out if you can hear me. You need to keep practising this, go out into the world and do your job."*

I felt confused and shocked. I couldn't believe I was talking to a snake, so I asked, *"Can I see you?"*

The snake answered, *"No, rather not. Your friend is afraid of snakes, and I don't want to scare her."*

I felt even more confused. My friend had never told me she was afraid of snakes, and here we were in the Australian bush. I simply said, *"Okay."*

The snake then replied, *"That was all. Just wanted to hear you and confirm you can hear me. Now go off and do your job."*

And that was it – he seemed to be going away.

My friend was looking at me strangely, and asked what had just happened. She said my face looked weird.

I asked her, *"Are you afraid of snakes?"*

Not a second later, she turned white as a ghost, and jumped up – looking around scared, and asking where the snake was.

That was my validation. My absolute certainty that I hadn't dreamt it, and wasn't making it up.

I explained to her that there is no snake around, or at least, not anymore, so she relaxed a little bit.

I told her what had happened and that the snake was also compassionate towards her fear.

We both sat quietly for a while in amazement.

Deep in my heart, I knew the job ahead of me. I knew the snake was absolutely right, and I had just discovered my purpose: connecting soul beings – animals and humans – to reunite them, reconnect them, enabling the creation of a harmonious and loving life together here on earth.

After we ate and rested, we continued with our walk. A few minutes later, and in an Aussie accent, there was a lizard calling me full of excitement. *"Hey, can you see me? Can you see me?"* When I acknowledged that I saw him on the tree, he was satisfied and just wandered off. I was again both shocked and amazed. Yet this time, with a sense of excitement.

Learning to talk with the animals

When I came home from that life-changing bushwalk, I opened the door and entered my house. Rosie and Toby ran towards me, as usual filled with excitement that I was home. Then Toby stopped and went very quiet. He sat in front of me, and stared. He held my gaze for a while and I felt like a waterfall of words and excitement came over me. He said he could finally tell me everything he ever wanted, as he could sense that I could hear and feel him. He didn't stop talking! That is, until I told him to slow down, because this was the first time it had happened, and I needed time to understand, adjust, and become comfortable with this new skill. He was so excited and happy – I couldn't believe it!

Rosie was also excited, but she was more reserved in sharing what she wanted me to know.

To this day, Toby always talks and is happy to do so. Rosie is more selective around what she is sharing, and waits until she is ready.

In the following months I went searching for teachers and information about talking to animals. I found several sources which gave me different tools to practise, and I learned how to listen to animals, resulting in two certificates and grand expansion of my skills.

As I learned more about how I could hear the animals, I was amazed at how much I learned from them and how lovely and relaxing it could be to have a conversation with an animal.

Initially I practised only with Rosie and Toby, discovering the differences in their energy, personalities, and how they communicate with me. For example, Toby is very relaxed and his energy reflects that. He is a sook, very dependent, and his energy is extremely mellow. Toby is also an old soul, and very wise.

Rosie, on the other hand, has a higher and more energetic vibration, and comes through with lots of excitement. She is more pedantic and not always willing to communicate. She will indicate to me if she is ready to talk. She is also a very independent dog and likes to do things her own way, yet on the other hand she is very supportive towards Toby and us. In many ways, her personality mirrors mine.

I always speak with animals with gratitude and respect.

I talk to Rosie and Toby every day, whether out loud or in my mind. It is so much fun! It has also helped me to understand them much better. For example, Rosie tells me whether she is hungry or not and what she wants to eat. She also tells me what she wants to do; go to the park or just a walk around the block, chill and relax. Rosie is a wealth of wisdom, advice and support. Toby is my guardian, my gatekeeper.

Talking with animals is an intuitive process, and usually happens via telepathy. Of course they can hear our voice, but don't necessarily understand our language. What's important is what we project to them, including our energy. That is how they understand what we are saying. They can send us a picture, a smell, a colour, or words via telepathy. We receive this only when we are tuned in to them.

Animals live from their hearts. They are connected to spirit at a higher vibrational level[7] and give absolute and complete unconditional love. It gives us such a great feeling to see our own beloved animal approach us, wanting us to receive their love.

Whether animals have a specific message for us or just want to have a conversation, communicating with our animal friends is an enjoyable and therapeutic experience.

Animals are so wise and have many stories and much information to share, so it is important for me to share how you can connect and listen to them. Whether you have a pet in your family, you are a foster animal human guardian[8], have animals on your farm, or rescue animals from misery and abuse, everyone can learn this wonderful and important skill.

Hello? Can You Hear Me?

Over the years, I have spoken with birds, dogs, cats, goannas, horses, guinea pigs, cows, sheep, koalas, kangaroos, and certain insects.

I feel so honoured to be able to communicate with animals. It feels great to hear the different voices and feel the different energies.

I am loving it, and I am sure you will too!!

Loving whispers of a furry kind

My encounters with animals

Animals are able to teach us a lot about the environment we live in. They also teach us about ourselves as human beings, as Soul beings, and as spirit in this human form. Most importantly, they teach us about why and how we are all connected to each other.

Each one of us has a Soul, and is connected to Source energy. We are all sentient beings, both humans and animals. I know from experience that plants and trees hold energy the same way as we do, and can provide us with healing and wisdom. It is this healing and wisdom that animals show and provide us, through the same Universal energy.

It is sometimes claimed that people are in our lives because we either learn from them, or we teach them. Therefore it is no coincidence that we make such personal connections in our lives. The same goes for animals. It doesn't matter how small the animal is. Whether it has fur, a snakeskin, an alligator skin, or feathers. It doesn't matter what animal is around us, they have a reason for being with us at any given point in time. This reason becomes more apparent the more we connect and engage.

It is very important for us to know why animals are with us, and why they are so eager to connect through animal communication.

An animal might be in pain, or perhaps have other problems which interfere with their everyday life.

Maybe we are not feeding them properly, or *we* are not behaving properly. It's crucial we learn how to listen to them.

I must tell you that nine times out of ten, when I work with an animal, they have something to say about the human guardians around them or the family they live with. Sometimes it's not easy to hear what the animal has to say about us, as it may not be all positive. I have learned that a particular animal can manifest my working with them in such a way that the human guardian actually finds me and engages with me.

Behaviour can change for an animal as *we* need to pay attention to something that is not working in our own lives.

Let me share some examples of this.

Spirit, the leopard

Perhaps one of the best-known stories of animal communication comes through Anna Breytenbach. Anna is a very well-known animal communicator from South Africa.

Diablo was a black leopard, rescued from a zoo in Europe, where he'd been abused, and brought to a lion rehabilitation sanctuary in Africa. The founder of this sanctuary had a very special relationship with his wild cats, and the aggression which Diablo displayed was something he didn't know how to deal with. Even after six months in his new safe-haven, Diablo's behaviour hadn't improved.

Anna was called in for two reasons. Firstly, to prove that animal communication was a valid form of interaction with animals, and secondly, to assist Diablo. The sanctuary founder was very sceptical towards animal communication, and it took some convincing to allow her anywhere near the enclosure.

Within moments of meeting Anna, Diablo calmed down, and exchanged information which his new translator could not possibly have known beforehand. Having convinced Diablo's caretakers of her genuine ability, Anna went on to explain the panther's needs.

Renamed "Spirit", this special panther's behaviour changed entirely after that encounter, and he went on to have a happy life at the sanctuary.

Not only that, but Spirit's caretaker realised his special relationship with the other cats was actually a form of animal communication, and he was already connecting without even knowing it.

Audrey the cat

A few years ago, I worked with a friend's cat, Audrey. This beautiful cat formed part of a loving family. She was mature, and usually very friendly, yet kept to herself. She had her favourite spots around the house, and was living out her life in a gentle way.

However, one day this suddenly changed. Audrey became quite aggressive towards people, something she would otherwise never do. In particular, she showed aggression towards one member of the household. They couldn't figure out what was going on with her, and asked me if I could help.

I connected with Audrey, and my, what a fussy eater she is! The main issue though, was that one particular family member was drinking alcohol at night, and she didn't relate to that very well. She didn't feel that it was a good thing for that person to do, because it had a negative effect on him. Being aggressive was her way of letting him know "*I don't like what you are doing, you need to stop this.*"

Sometimes I provide Reiki healing during an animal communication session. This form of energy healing helps the animal to calm down, reduces aches and pains, and can help to balance energy levels as well as reduce inflammation. I also apply Reiki when I want to 'see' what the animal is sharing with me. I receive the images directly from the animal through the energy in my hands.

I provided some Reiki healing for Audrey during our session, and she loved it! Audrey became very mellow and her energy shifted from being angry, upset, and annoyed, to relaxed and comfortable. She even went outside and lay in front of the window in the sun. Apparently, she hadn't done that for a long time.

After we learned of Audrey's reason for her behaviour, it was shared with the members of her family. She started to settle down after the person in question started to change his behaviour.

This story is one of the reasons I am so passionate about connecting with animals; we can help each other.

Three furry children move overseas

Another story I'd love to share is that of a family who moved from Australia to the United States. Ashley and her partner were very concerned about the animals moving with them: Floyd and Pearl, their two dogs, and Walter, the cat.

Ashley contacted me as she wanted to be absolutely sure the animals were aware of the move, and wanted advice on how she could support them so they'd have the best experience she could give them.

Ashley explained to me what was going to happen during the animals' travels, which people were going to help them each step of the way and what they could expect. This included packing up the house in Sydney, check-ups with the vet, boarding the plane, and driving to their new home in the United States.

I connected with all three animals and explained to them what they could expect during their travels, as per Ashley's expectations. I visualised for them where they were going, how they were going to get there, and who was supporting them during their trip. In particular, I also asked how we could best support them, so they have the best experience possible, with the least amount of stress.

All the animals were extremely grateful for the explanations and images I provided them. Part of this information they already knew as Ashley had indeed talked to them, and they also picked up on the energy from both human guardians.

The main support they requested was Rescue Remedy and ginger, both useful and natural remedies used for stress relief and travel-related nausea. They also told me what items they wanted to travel with, in particular on the plane, and their expectations of their new country. I also told them that when they left the airplane, they would go on a car trip to drive to their new home.

The end result was that all the fur family arrived safe and sound, and now live happily in their new home.

Not only was this a great experience for the animals, but also for Ashley and her husband. It was wonderful for them to be in a position to help the animals and give them what they were asking for. We all wanted to be sure they had minimal stress and the most comfort during this big change.

Shadow embraces healing

One of the best experiences in my journey with animals has been here in Australia, on a farm in the state of Victoria.

The farm had five rescue horses at the time, of which one was a brumby; an Australian wild horse. I've visited the farm several times, but I will never forget the first time I arrived and met the horses.

After I'd settled in, I went out to the paddocks. The house was in the middle of eleven acres of land, surrounded by the Australian bush. The air was filled with fresh smells of eucalyptus trees and flowers, and I could feel the history of the land and the animals residing on it. I sensed this was a sacred place.

When I walked on the grass I immediately grounded myself. I felt calm, and at one with nature. I tuned into anything and everything around me.

I turned around to look at the horses. The first thing I saw was Trooper the brumby in the furthest paddock, lifting his head towards me with his ears straight up. The four horses in the second paddock did the same. All five were looking at me with great interest, and I could feel curiosity, excitement, and love coming right at me.

Then all of a sudden, Trooper started running out of the paddock, onto the path alongside the other paddocks, galloping towards me. He couldn't wait to come and meet me! But the gate was closed. We ran towards the gate to open it, and as he came through he was all over me, greeting me with the same level of excitement as a dog. He didn't jump on me though, thank goodness!

The other horses joined in and ran toward me too. We all had an amazing time, greeting and getting to know one another.

I had never experienced anything like that, and neither had Mae Lee, the caretaker, who said she'd never seen anything like it.

The next day, I went out to see all the horses and asked who wanted my help, healing, or to have a chat. Shadow, the only female, remained in front of me while the others walked away, and I knew she was the one who needed the healing that day.

Shadow had been rescued, and never allowed any strangers to approach her, so it was very unusual for her to wait for me and ask for help. Shadow suffered navicular disease in her body. She was in a lot of pain and she knew I could help her, so I started working with her and gave her lots of Reiki healing. This healing helped her pain to be significantly reduced and the negative energy in her body was removed. Inflammation was also diminished, although not completely removed. The stiffness in her hind legs was less than before our session started. Shadow needed many more sessions to be completely released from her symptoms.

The beauty of this healing was not only about helping Shadow and understanding what she was going through, but also that she had the support of the other horses in the herd, and the farm cat too.

Both Mae Lee and I noticed the other horses standing around us in a circle. They enjoyed observing the healing, and were holding space for the beautiful connection that was taking place between Shadow and me. From that moment I was more convinced than ever that horses are incredible spiritual beings, healers, and teachers.

To see a video of my connection with Shadow, use this link: www.biancadereus.com/animal-healing

I could share many more stories with you, but I would love nothing more than for you to create your own stories, through communicating with animals.

May I see through your eyes?

There are different ways we can find out what animals experience, think and feel. For example, we can observe their behaviour, be present with them, and pat them. To talk to an animal and really connect with them, we might hear their voice, feel what they feel, see what they show us, or we can even pick up information by simply touching them gently.

When we connect with animals through distance, we bring our frequency to the same level as theirs, and then we tune in and listen to what they have to say. Let's take it a step further: What would you say if I told you that we can *see through their eyes* as well? As in... almost literally?

When we connect with an animal and are not in their direct proximity to view their surroundings, we can ask to see through their eyes and have them show us around.

Sounds crazy right? So, I thought as well, but it's happened to me on many occasions, one of which I'd love to share with you.

Years ago, when I was learning about animal communication, I met a beautiful woman who lives on Kangaroo Island in South Australia. She was in Sydney attending a conference, and we connected and started talking about our dogs. She then asked if I could tune into her dog. I connected with her dog and asked permission.

I asked the dog, *"Can you please show me around your house, and I'll describe it, so your human guardian knows I am connecting with you?"* The dog was more than willing and was very enthusiastic.

I brought my energy to a higher vibrational level, higher than usual, and this enabled me to merge with her energy. She allowed me to meld, and it was the strangest yet most exciting feeling ever.

I felt everything bobbing around and moving. I realised I was merged with her, and she was running around her property in the yard. I was bouncing around and then I could see: I described the garden, the spot where she sleeps, her water bowl, the colours, the back of the house, boots in front of the door - everything. The woman was astonished, and so was I! What an insightful experience.

Ever since that encounter, I ask animals if I am allowed to see where they are, and that is how they respond. It is such an amazing way to describe their immediate surroundings.

I'll give you another example:

Mitch, the cockatoo

A client contacted me because her cockatoo, Mitch, was very out of sorts. She was biting and pulling feathers, as well as screaming a lot. When I talked with Mitch, she explained that she was unhappy with her surroundings and certain people living close to her. She showed me where she lived: her enclosure, the house, the backyard and the broader surroundings. She identified that the energy was not well; very out of balance, dark and grey and very high-pressured. My client was aware, but felt there was not much to do about this. We worked out a few small steps which both my client and Mitch could take to improve the situation. Mitch was given a warm place in her enclosure with fabric and hay. Her enclosure was moved to a different area and we listened to her requests and stories. She stopped plucking and biting herself. The screaming is still ongoing, but that has to do with the environment, which my client has been cleansing energetically. Slowly but surely the shifts are happening.

Allowing animals to merge with my energy so I can see through their eyes has not only helped me to know what may contribute to the animal's feelings, but also to find missing or lost animals. This merged vision helps me describe where they are, and it has helped me locate dogs interstate, and reunite them with their human guardians.

That takes animal communication to a whole new level!

I invite you to reflect on what you have observed in your pet or other animals recently, which you can now recognise as communication. Jot down your notes and thoughts:

_____

_____

_____

_____

_____

_____

_____

_____

_____

_____

_____

_____

_____

_____

_____

_____

_____

_____

_____

_____

_____

_____

Honouring some of the beautiful animal souls
I have worked with over the years...

"Goodbyes are only for those who love with their eyes.

Because for those who love with heart and soul, there is no such thing as separation.

Your body is away from me but there is a window open from my heart to yours."

~Rumi

Crossing the rainbow bridge

From grief to peace

Death is often a subject we don't want to talk or think about. It is too painful, yet so important to discuss, as it's an integral part of our lives. Our beloved animals are with us for only a short period of time.

When an animal crosses over and leaves us, we like to think they cross a colourful rainbow bridge. Us humans imagine that animals group together and cross this beautiful bridge to the after-life, starting with a happy, peaceful journey.

There is so much joy, happiness, and fun in working with animals each day and hearing their stories. I love relaying their anecdotes to their human guardians so that I can help them. It is an incredible honour that animals trust me to be their voice, share their feelings, and be the conduit for their messages, even during difficult times.

The flip side of this work is that animals also share with me *when* they leave their life on earth, and move on to the spirit realms, crossing that rainbow bridge.

My experience tells me that animals know when and where they are going. Animals let us know that they are preparing or are ready to go very soon. They also let us know if they require assistance or if they'll just fall asleep and not wake up. They will show me where they are going in colours and images, and tell me who is waiting to accompany them on their new journey.

These are the tough messages I have to share. The pain animals are in, the suffering they go through, and then receiving that phone call from a client telling me that their beloved pet has indeed crossed the bridge.

It deeply saddens me, but that is my human side. The grief my client shares, I feel intensely. My spirit side shows me that the animals are safe, feeling joy and freedom, no longer in pain, and happy with their friends, family, and loved ones in the spirit realm.

I seek comfort in the fact that I can help an animal to cross over, and share their last wishes and words with their human guardians. Most animals are extremely grateful and thank us for looking after them, and for the wonderful life they have had with us.

We can help to keep them comfortable and let them know what they will experience during and after crossing the rainbow bridge. We can let them know we love them and will never forget them – and that makes me happy.

Sometimes, there is an animal I've worked with and have become attached to, and it takes longer to accept that they are indeed gone. And that is okay.

I have to remind myself that I am human too. I can experience the grief for a little bit, and then I can check in with the animal a few days or weeks later and find out they are okay and still around, if that is what they choose to do. Then there is joy again, and happiness.

Because people want me to connect with their loved ones, I have the great honour and pleasure of sharing with them that they are alright, and can pass on any other messages they have. We all feel better knowing this. It helps us to release our grief, experience peace, and understand that we can keep our beloved pet in our hearts forever.

The Souls of animals are still around us. They are connected with us and also help us to find a new pet if we so choose.

When people want me to connect with their pet who has passed on, I have to explain that it is not up to me to make that connection. If that Soul wants to communicate with us, then they need to make contact with us. We cannot call them back. They have work to do on the other side, or they may have reincarnated, and therefore it can be dangerous calling them back. We also don't want to run the risk of them staying here, possibly stuck on the Earth plane.

Sure, we can think of them often and remember the great times we had together, but we can never call them back.

I do have animal Souls (and human Souls) coming to me after they have passed over, and usually only to share a message they hadn't been able to share before they left.

There is one particular dog who comes to me on occasion to help me with other animals who are ready to pass over. This dog lived with my best friend, and was very close to me. Every time we saw each other, she used to say that she was "*home*". She passed away at a very young age. We had a close relationship and a deep connection.

Since her passing, she has become a guide to animals ready to pass over; the ones who seek my help with their transition. I am so blessed to have her assist these animals. She shares with them where they are going and who will be there for them. She sometimes helps them with a safe passage, if the animal is scared or doesn't know what to expect.

Teamwork is a wonderful thing!

Animals and grief

It's not only us humans who experience grief; animals experience it too. We need to be there to help them, and allow them to move through it. They experience the same feelings and processes as humans do.

A lot of us don't realise that animals have deep feelings, and also suffer from grief when a family member passes over. We have a job to help them with this. You may have seen this happen. For example, I remember seeing an image of a dog who lay in front of the coffin of his human guardian in the church, saying his last good-byes.

I have seen animals who know that a family member is not coming back home and yet, they still have hope that they will walk through the door. The hope comes from the fact that we did not take the time to talk to our animal family members about the departure and explain that the person or animal is not coming back. It also comes from the animal being able to sense the departed soul around them, as the energy is still there. This is because animals always sense our energy first, not the body we are in.

The same as we would for our human children, we need to talk to our animals about the departure. How it happened, when it happened, and what is going to happen next. We must tell them that we understand they may experience sadness, grief, and pain for the loss. Really take the time to explain the process, and reassure them that it is okay for them to feel these feelings. Allow them to go through the process.

"How do I explain that?" I hear you ask. Well, you just talk to your pet as if you are talking to another person. Use your own words to describe the event, and at the same time comfort your pet. This process will also help you with your grief, as you are not alone going through this, and that is sometimes useful to know.

It's important to let our animals know that we are there for them, with full support if they want a cuddle, attention, the extra long walk, or even that extra biscuit as comfort for their feelings. Nurture them as gently as you'd nurture yourself and your other family members during these difficult times.

When our animals have a solid understanding and know we care about their feelings too, they are able to support us in return, and help us with our own grief. You can see this happen, as the animals will nudge us, come up to comfort us, and try to cheer us up by engaging in play to move our energies towards positivity.

If you sense that your animal is sad or off-colour, ask them questions, give them some more attention, and observe their behaviour. This will help you to find out what they are asking of you. You will intuitively know what is going on and be able to support them.

Rosie and Toby

This is very hard to write about, and I am sharing the following information as it helps you to further understand how you might *know* your pet is about to transition to the non-physical world.

In the midst of finalising this book, my dog Rosie passed away. The last few weeks before her passing, she showed signs of illness. Not once during that period did she indicate the severity of her pain or the intensity of her illness. We visited the vet, who sent me home with painkillers and antibiotics for her, as the blood tests didn't really confirm anything apart from a bowel infection. Considering her age, we just wanted her to be comfortable. A week later we returned to the vet, as Rosie had not improved. In fact, she had lost more weight.

I continued to talk to her, but she wasn't sharing much with me. The morning I brought her back to the vet, I engaged my friend and fellow animal communicator, Amanda Powers, to talk with Rosie. She said that Rosie wasn't in a lot of physical pain, but she was in a lot of emotional pain, as she knew she didn't have much time left to spend with us. She wasn't ready to say her goodbyes, and neither were we. She confirmed that she knew her body was giving up. We allowed the vet to take x-rays to confirm her actual physical state. Rosie was riddled with cancer in her lungs and bowels. And so, the most difficult signature ever ended up on a piece of paper, a few hours later at the vet's office.

Rosie fell asleep peacefully in my arms, with her head snuggled up in my neck.

You see, when you are in an emotional state yourself, connections with animals may not occur. This could be because you close this off yourself, or, in Rosie's case, they don't want to talk as they know it will hurt you. Therefore, having an 'interpreter' such as an animal communicator is recommended.

Rosie's brother, Toby was supported throughout the passing of Rosie. We told him what was happening when she was sick, to the point of her leaving the house and allowing Toby and Rosie to say goodbye to each other. He knew already what was going on, but to have it confirmed by us allowed him to process it, say goodbye, and support us.

Sadly, Toby is also preparing to cross over. He is nearly fifteen years old - 21st September is his shared birthday with Rosie - and he has been deteriorating very quickly in the last couple of months. Last year he suffered two minor strokes, resulting in vestibular disease, making him very unstable on his feet. This seemed to have eased off for a while, but it has now become more prominent. He has arthritis in his hind legs, and his hearing is getting worse. All these are signs of ageing. One of his front legs is now also getting limp, and his head is tilting more and more towards the left.

At night, he roams the house, very restless, and he cries most of the time. Often I get out of bed to calm him down, take him outside for him to do his business and then settle him back in his own bed until he falls asleep.

In addition, he is still grieving for Rosie and often looks up expecting to see her, and walks over to her favourite places to look around. Lots of cuddles, support and conversations are happening.

I've asked him many times how I can help, and if he needs assistance to cross over. I've received messages that he just needs me to comfort him and he will not need assistance as he will just fall asleep.

One night, he was crying so loudly and deeply from within his body that I woke up feeling very scared. I took him to the vet, as I felt so much pain coming from his body. The vet was shocked to see him in the state he was. The vet confirmed my worst fear; Toby has days, perhaps weeks left on earth. Even though I am not a fan of medication, I feel I need to help Toby to be as comfortable as possible. He still does *not* want any assistance. I have even called upon a friend of mine, also an animal communicator, to tune into Toby and she's confirmed what I already know. He's told her he doesn't want to leave yet, as

I will be in pain, and that he is preparing and will just fall asleep.

We have put him on painkillers, anti-inflammatory medication and antibiotics. He is still wagging his tail, is in good spirits and eats like he's never been fed before. But his body is slowly shutting down.

I tell him every day I love him and that when he is ready I am willing to let him go, and I will be there for him, so he can cross over safely and with love.

Every day, I provide him with even more love and care than I have ever given him. Just so he knows, he has my permission to go.

As Toby is going through his elderly journey and, dealing with his sister's passing, we are now even more focused on spending time with him and truly feeling blessed for every day he is still here with us.

In memory:

Place a photo of your pet(s)
to keep your connection open with them and
remember them fondly and with love

Connecting to your inner self

Letting your intuition guide you

Hello? Can you hear me? wasn't just a question for me to pay attention to the snake. I now know it is also a question that we need to ask ourselves regularly. As humans we don't often listen to gut feelings, inner voice, or the things around us, let alone the animal kingdom.

When we are tuned into ourselves, we're better equipped to tune into animals, and I must emphasise the importance of caring for our own wellbeing.

Listening starts by listening to your S.E.L.F, your Inner Guidance, and your Soul.

Why are we not listening? Why don't we take time out to be with ourselves, to allow us to listen to what we have to say and to love ourselves? There is so much information and knowledge to share with ourselves. We are all such wise, beautiful, bright, and wonderful Beings!

All too often people ask me; *"What do you think I should do next? Where do you see me right now?"*

Well, it is certainly not up to me to tell you what to do next. Of course, I can give you my humble opinion, observations, guidance, and suggestions, but I strongly recommend for you to be quiet, and listen to your S.E.L.F. Ask your S.E.L.F the questions. You DO have all the answers.

Sometimes we just need someone to nudge us in the right direction and give us the tools and the know-how, so we can listen to our S.E.L.F: our Soul Eternal Love Flame. That nudge might come from me, but it also appears from within your own heart, or from spirit guides.

It makes me wonder, why are we humans not living our lives from the heart all the time? Why are we not treating ourselves and each other with kindness and why are we not showing each other unconditional love? Aren't we part of this world, the animal and plant kingdoms? Why do we believe we are superior to other animals? If anything, the animals are superior to us, and we have a lot to learn from them.

Years ago, I met an amazing woman who didn't realise how beautiful she was, inside and out. We'll call her Cynthia.

For over fifteen years, Cynthia had been surrounded by people who didn't appreciate her, never complimented her, and always looked at the things she wasn't doing. She had lost a lot of confidence and just wanted to hide from the world.

She searched for me, as she had heard I could help her.

Initially I let her talk, as I felt she just needed to be listened to. Following her outpouring of words and emotion, the first thing I told her was that she is a wonderful Soul, and a beautiful being. I also told her to stay true to herself and to look after her own wellbeing. She mentioned that no one had ever given her such praise or self-care advice. She was so amazed that those words could have such a deep impact on her soul.

We then went through a few exercises to help her connect to her inner self, ground her energies, and anchor the words I said and the ones she had come up with herself into her body, so she could feel the beautiful Soul she is and reconnect to her Spirit.

We also worked on a few limiting beliefs, the thoughts she had about herself that were holding her back from what she wanted and prevented her from truly connecting to her core being.

The reason I share this with you is that so many of the people I speak with don't believe in themselves. They don't find themselves beautiful, or love themselves. Animals guide us to love ourselves unconditionally. This is the only way we can truly live and serve ourselves, others, and the rest of the world.

Clear the fear

I feel sad when I learn that some people stay in an environment or situation because fear does not allow them to move away. Part of what Cynthia was experiencing was fear based, hence the limiting beliefs she held.

So many people have not been shown how they can remove or reduce fear, so as to continue their own journey, their own way forward, and invite positivity into their life.

Fear is merely "False Expectations Appearing Real", or as Gabrielle Bernstein says in her book *The Universe Has your Back (Hay House 2016)*: "*F*** Everything and Run*".

Running is not going to be beneficial, although it's the easiest option. You are not facing the fear or understanding it when you run.

When we are afraid, we expect that something which scares us is about to happen. Something that appears to be in the future is making us uncomfortable and is often the worst-case scenario of the outcome we are expecting. That creates anxiety, procrastination, and feelings of being stuck. And that is certainly not helping you in your life.

I'd like to invite you to look at fear as something that has *not* happened, as it's not a reality, and to take inspired action, so you have what you desire. Then imagine what it may feel like if you do have what you desire? This allows you to bring the feeling of already having achieved your desires into the *now*. When this happens, fear fades into the background.

I'd love to share two exercises you can apply to fear, and any other negative emotions:

Exercise one:

When you feel fear, face it. Say in your mind: *"Hey, what am I doing? That thing I think is going to happen, hasn't happened yet. So, what is the worst that can happen to me?"*

Once you've come up with what the worst thing is, then ask what the next worst thing is, and the next... Once you know all these, then breathe it out, and say: *"I would love to experience loving relationships or have abundant wealth in my life, and I will feel happy, loved and free when I have it."*
Relationships and wealth are only two examples of what you might desire, and you can replace these with anything which works for you.

Observe and tune into these feelings. Bring them into your body and energy *now*.

When you bring those desired feelings and experiences into your body, you will become aligned with these new feelings, and you are able to take inspired action to realise your desire.

Exercise two:

This exercise was taught to me by Shawna Pelton, Transformation Expert (www.shawnapelton.com) and I love this one too. She calls this "the F it exercise". When you are triggered by fear, anger, sadness, anxiety or any other negative emotions, you F it: *feel* it, *forgive* it and *free* it.

Feel the feeling: the moment you feel the trigger, you feel it emotionally, physically, mentally and spiritually. Feel the feeling really deeply. Don't hide from it, don't deny it, don't judge it and make it all wrong and criticise yourself, but feel it like you have never been with that feeling before.

Forgive it: forgive everything and everyone involved with the feeling, then feel the forgiveness. Say something like "I forgive myself for having these feelings. I forgive the perpetrator for this predicament." In this moment, forgive and feel the forgiveness deeply.

Free it: free the feeling by not entertaining the impulse any longer; release it. Make a new decision by doing something different, create a new energetic release.

Play around with these two exercises, and see which one resonates with you, and remember: You *are* a beautiful, wonderful, attractive, magnificent, loved, capable, amazing human being. You *deserve* to have the best and most loving experiences in your life.

I invite you to start loving and trusting yourself. Believe that you can feel and have that which you desire.

Make a note below and share with me what you experience with these exercises.

The power in what I do is to
focus on the heart and
remain in alignment
to experience conscious
communication.

This will bring you harmony in
perfect flow and from
a place of unconditional love:
true soul to soul connection.

The importance of connection

Now, I don't know where you are in life with your beliefs, and this may be a little bit far-fetched for you, however, I am going to share this concept anyway. Besides, you probably wouldn't be reading this book if you didn't already know a little bit about spirit abilities and the spirit realms.

To prepare for connecting with animals, we must first connect to ourselves by finding an opening to our heart.

This connection allows us to hear, feel and understand ourselves and our inner core. Connecting to your heart opens up your heart chakra[9], allowing you to feel love, first for yourself, and then for all other beings and all that is in the Universe.

A Chakra is one of seven energetic focal points in the body, each of them relating to a specific area of the body and its correlating organs and emotions. In energetic healing, a chakra may become blocked, which interferes with the physical or emotional health of that part of the body. The key to visualising your heart chakra (or any other chakra) is to picture it as a swirling wheel of energy.

Perhaps you have meditated before? Or maybe you have experienced stillness, if only for a few moments? And you may have experienced heightened senses, such as hearing, feeling or seeing. That is when you are connected to your heart and everything around you.

I personally love it when I am in a meditation, a walk along the beach, or in nature, and I am so connected, still, and at one with myself and everything around me. It's then I receive messages.

The messages are not just from myself, but from nature, animals and other beings...

Our guides

Have you ever felt you are not alone in the room? Or felt the sensation of someone standing behind you? I know, it's spooky, right? I am here to tell you that it is not spooky at all, especially when you know it is actually your Spirit Guide. Your Spirit Guide is here for you, ever present, letting you know that you are supported at all times.

"But, I am reading this book because I want to know about animal communication!"

Yes, that is correct, you will learn about animal communication, but I have a duty to explain your Spirit Guides to you, as they will play a vital role in animal communication.

Guides are non-earthly beings who have already lived a life (or more) on earth. They are in the spirit world, on a higher spiritual plane[10], providing us with guidance, wisdom, and support. They share and guide us based on their experience and what they know about us, and how they see our life unfold.

The spiritual plane is an energetic platform, where it's believed that souls and eternal forms exist. It is strongly connected with the birth and death cycle, and considered to be a place which exists beyond Earth and various astral planes. Traditionally, the spiritual plane might be known as heaven, or the celestial realm, and it is known as a place of great love, truth, and beauty. It is here our guides dwell, and from this place they provide the insight and guidance we need to truly connect with animals.

In my early teens I first learned that what I could always *sense* was one of my guides. I had always known I wasn't really alone and never really paid attention. During this time, I consciously connected with my guides for the first time, but then almost forgot about them and didn't really think much of them. They were just there, and without my realising, they always had been, helping me as friends would with everyday life and its challenges.

Only later in life, when I fully embraced my spiritual abilities and the connections with Spirit, Source and All That Is, did I research more into these topics.

One of the books that really helped me understand guides and how we can tap into them was called *Opening to Channel* (Sanaya Roman & Duane Packer, 1989)[11]. After reading that book I understood how to fully connect and work with my own spirit guides, some of whom have been with me all my life.

During one of my many meditations, I even asked my ever-present guide if he could show himself. (And yes, I always knew he was a he.) He showed up as if in a movie, right in front of my face.

This particular guide looked cheeky, and had a great sense of humour. He had a beard and a hat, and always came across as jovial - he still does. He introduced himself as one of my spiritual guides, Gideon, and told me that we have been together for a long time.

One day he mentioned that a certain meditation would help people to connect with their heart, and raise their vibrational energy. He also told me that it would help people to connect intuitively to animals, other people, and most importantly, to themselves. Gideon said this is part of the work I do; helping people reconnect to their Soul, their S.E.L.F. and to shine their light.

I am sharing this beautiful meditation with you here. It is called *"Connect to Your Heart"* and I lovingly invite you to practise this as often as you can.

Connect with your heart – a meditation

Let's get you into it! You will now prepare for communicating with animals. But most importantly, you will first connect deeply with your S.E.L.F.

In doing this exercise, you will feel the most intense love and energy you have ever felt before. This will raise your energetic vibration and open you up to Universal love and energy, to be able to:

- connect with your heart and your inner S.E.L.F.
- let go, relax and trust
- connect with your spirit guide(s)
- connect with whom you want to connect (both humans and animals)

I suggest you find a comfortable, private area, where you will not be interrupted and can take all the time you need. You can lie down or stay seated, as long as you are comfortable. This may be in your home, on the bed, or outside in nature.

1. Place your hand over your heart.
2. Close your eyes.
3. Breathe deeply into your heart, 5 breaths in, 5 breaths out.
4. Stay still for a moment after the last out breath, allowing the energy to surge through your body.
5. Visualise a green light around you, emanating directly from your heart, and white light

coming from above, through your crown chakra (the top of your head) into your heart.

6. Think of a person or animal you love absolutely and unconditionally, and allow that feeling of love to enter your heart.
7. Send love to them and be in that energy for a while, so you become more familiar with how this feels.

When you are ready you can slowly come back into the room, feel yourself physically present, and open your eyes.

Congratulations! You have connected with your inner self and someone else! Well done.

The same exercise is used when you want to talk with an animal. You get into the same energetic zone, send the green light directly from your heart to theirs, and ask for permission. When you have this, you can open the communication with an animal, which I'll describe in the next chapter.

Living from a place of unconditional love is all there is. When you live from this place you are in the flow, your flow. You shine your light for you and everyone and everything around you.

From this place you are a Being who experiences life to the fullest. You can experience abundance in love, health, joy, and wealth. You can encounter beautiful relationships and a beautiful life, and live in the way you choose.

From this space you will be whole, happy, joyful, at peace and one with All That Is.

And so, it is.

How did you go?

Write down what you experienced during the meditation.

_____

_____

_____

_____

_____

_____

_____

_____

_____

_____

_____

_____

_____

_____

_____

_____

_____

_____

_____

_____

_____

_____

_____

_____

I invite you to let me know about your experience. Contact details are in the back of the book.

The six steps

How to communicate with animals in a very practical way

Connection

Communicating with animals allows us to share words, images, feelings, emotions, and colours with them. The animals will share these titbits of information with you too.

The connection comes from a place of unconditional love via telepathy and intuitive connection, once we have permission to connect with the animal. They too have boundaries!

Remember the story about Spirit the leopard? In this case, the caretaker of the sanctuary was able to learn to communicate with the big cats, especially after witnessing the huge change in Spirit.

Following are six steps to help you connect in a very practical way, and includes the meditation you have already practised earlier on.

Are you ready?

SIX STEPS to connecting
with ANIMALS.

ONE
Find yourself a quiet place at home, or outdoors. A place where you are free from interruptions. For example, you may have a quiet meditation corner in the house, or a favourite spot in a park or on the beach.

TWO
Remember the "Connect with Your Heart" mediation I shared with you in the previous chapter? Use that here to connect to the animal you wish to speak with.

THREE

Now that you have established a connection with your S.E.L.F, imagine sending the green light directly to your pet or any other animal you wish to talk with. The green light represents unconditional love, from your heart to the heart centre of the animal.

FOUR

Ask for permission to connect and have a conversation. Introduce yourself. Some people receive this permission by hearing the animal saying "yes", or the animal showing you a picture of love and approval, or by feeling an intense hug. It is different for everyone, and I invite you to take note of what it is for you.

FIVE

Start by asking questions and patiently wait for the answer, which you will write down or record in audio. The information will present itself through words, images or feelings, and will come in very quickly, so it's important to record it and not analyse it! Make sure you also ask the animal if there is anything you can do to help them (or to help yourself). Do not force the connection as this will block the information flow between the two of you.

SIX

Now that you have received the information, you THANK your pet for the connection and share how grateful you are for this. Next, you create a simple action based on the information you received. Schedule these action items and work consistently on them., Keep your pet up to date every step of the way. Animals will continue to let us know what we need to do. After a while you might check-in with the animal, to find out how the action steps have made a difference, and when successful, if there is anything else you can do together.

Congratulations! You've spoken with an animal for the first time!

How did you go? What did you feel? What information did you receive?

If you haven't received information or felt that you weren't able to connect, please don't feel bad or worried. It's all good. You are learning a new skill, so be patient. Practising these steps over and over is the best thing you can do. You will absolutely be able to do this. Trust, patience and practise.

_____

_____

_____

_____

_____

_____

_____

_____

_____

_____

_____

_____

_____

_____

I am so keen to find out how you went!! Contact details can be found in the back of this book, let me know what you experienced.

Action plan

Most of the time you will receive so much information from animals that your head will spin.

My preferred way to record information is by audio recording. The information comes through me so quickly that I don't have the speed of writing to keep up with it.

The second I receive the answers, I verbalise them and it's then recorded. The information is then in its purest, raw and most authentic form, without filtering, judgement, or editing.

It's important I send the audio file to my clients, as they can then listen to the conversation as many times as they wish. Each time they listen, they will pick up new or different information.

Part of the information we receive are steps we need to implement, so as to make positive changes in our lives. This may be to help your pet, another animal, yourself, or other people.

These steps are important, as when they are not taken, things stay stagnant and don't change.

I invite you to write your action steps:

_____

_____

_____

_____

_____

_____

_____

_____

_____

_____

_____

_____

_____

_____

_____

_____

_____

_____

_____

_____

_____

_____

_____

_____

_____

_____

_____

_____

Toby

Rosie

Is my tail in the right place?

Observing how our animal friends behave

Animals have a reason for their behaviour, and before it can be altered or improved, animal communication allows us to understand why that animal is behaving in a certain way. We need to go deeper into their behaviour and what it brings the animal in that moment.

By understanding this concept, we can implement strategies together to improve the behaviour. By together, I mean both the animal and the human guardian. When both are willing to adjust, then behaviour improves.

Animals understand us. They want us to understand what goes on for them, and use their behaviour to try and explain this.

Sure, sometimes it's just stubbornness, or in the worst instance, pure aggression. What I have learned is that most animals change their behaviour because we need to pay attention to them, and ultimately to ourselves.

Animals rely on us to help with feeding, outdoor time, warmth or cooling down, and general care. They also rely on us doing the right thing by them, and they know they can help us be the best human being we can be, if only we pay attention!

I am certainly not an animal behaviourist. What I know, I have learned through talking with animals and observing how they can change instantly when we have a conversation. I have taken the time to understand what they go through, and why. When the change is not immediate or consistent, then an animal behaviourist can help, especially when I explain why the animals is behaving in a certain way. Working together is then much easier. If there is a need for a behaviourist, then such a person is invited into the team.

Your pet is your mirror

Do you observe your pet and identify any persistent behaviours that irritate you? Well pay attention; your pet is telling you something.

Previously I spoke about animals telling me the reasons they behave in a certain way, and that this may be a result of our own behaviour. We also need to observe our animals more closely, rather than talking to them, punishing them, or ignoring them.

I believe that some behaviour should not be tolerated, and is not the right way the animals should be. Such behaviour might include barking for no reason, sulking, following you, looking at you all the time, not eating, or perhaps presenting with the same aches and pains you also experience.

When you have a dog suffering anxiety, a cat who is shying away from humans, or a bird plucking feathers from their body, then we need to address this with and for our pet, and also look at ourselves and ask:

"What am I doing that might create this behaviour?"

"What is happening in our direct environment to create this behaviour?"

"What can we do to change that?"

Once we recognise this, and trust me, it's sometimes not easy to acknowledge, we can implement the right changes for ourselves and our animals.

Sometimes, it pushes us to connect back to ourselves, do a stocktake of our life; where we are at and what our next steps are.

The important thing here is to not just acknowledge it, but to actually implement the changes required.

Audrey the cat was behaving so aggressively because one of the people in the household was drinking excessively after work. That started to affect not only him, but also the other people in the household. Once he recognised this, he started taking steps to reduce his alcohol intake, having tea instead. This changed his behaviour for the better, and the family was happier for it as well as Audrey. She became her happy self again.

For our crazy cat people, here is another example of this – I can't let this example pass you by!

Rami, the cat with the keyboard fetish

Rami was an eight-year-old cat who lived for cuddles and belly rubs. His normally docile behaviour changed over the course of a few weeks, when he began sitting on his guardian's computer keyboard. If she moved him, he would either jump straight back up, or turn and bite her. This was very uncharacteristic behaviour for him.

Rami's guardian tried all the tricks in the book to distract him, but he insisted on sitting on the keyboard or pushing it off the desk.

As she worked from home, it was important to Rami's mum that this behaviour stopped. At her wits' end, she called me for help.

Rami was finally able to explain that the work his guardian was doing was actually not suited to her, and she was doing herself a disservice by continuing. This was confusing and alarming for her, as she was working three different roles from home, and was uncertain which one he meant!

I was able to clarify this for her, and she began to pay attention to when Rami was particularly persistent (and annoying!)

Within a month, she reduced her workload significantly, and Rami returned to his usual docile, snuggly self. He still lets her know when she is being distracted from what he sees as her "true work", but for the most part he picks a cushion near her desk and snores while she types.

This is yet another of my many examples of how our pets really do know what's best for us, and will do anything to try and let us know!

Our animals are our guides, our teachers, and our mirrors. They want us to be happy, fulfilled and at peace.

Thank you for looking after me

Our wellbeing helps us to better connect

Treat your body with love and devotion

One of the many things I am passionate about is looking after our bodies as much as we would for our animal friends. It may seem strange that I am talking about this, as this book is mostly about the connecting with animals. However, looking after ourselves, our body, is vital when we work with our spiritual and metaphysical skills, as well as when we are communicating with our animals friends and spirit.

Trust me, I am not a nutritionist or vet. Far from it! I can share this based on my own experience and what I have learned along the way from looking after this 47-year young body!

When you are eating, I'd like to invite you to ask yourself questions such as:

"How does my body feel after I've eaten a meal?"
"Does it feel satisfied?"
"Am I full of energy? Or do I feel lethargic and bloated, and experience aches and pains?"
"When was the last time I exercised or went for a walk?"

We are all living fast and feel we have no time, but looking after our physical body is the most important thing we can do, along with our spiritual and mindfulness activities.

It is very important to LISTEN and FEEL INTO your body every time you eat and move. Keep a journal and identify what foods and activities serve your body's optimum health and energy levels.

This is something I have been doing for a long time, and it has been a great way for me to understand what my body loves, and what I should keep doing as it feels best for my body. This exercise has also had a big influence on healing my body from disease - in particular plant-based nutrition - it really is a huge part of healing.

If you find that a certain type of food has a negative impact on your body, stay away from it for a while and see how you feel then. You don't put petrol in a diesel car, do you? The same goes for your body. Not every single body is designed to eat everything that is on offer, so do your body (and your spirit) a favour, and start to identify what makes your body THRIVE!

The same goes for our animals. They too need to eat the right food for their bodies. If you find that your pet has a reaction or experiences a negative impact from food, then change this for them.

All too often I talk to animals and they share with me that the first thing they want to change is what they eat. Us humans rarely take the time to research what the best food is for our beloved animals, when to feed them, and even when to have a rest day.

More often than not animals share with me that they are not being fed the right food. The number of animals who raise this issue is alarmingly high. About 7 out of 10 animals I work with mention nutrition as a point to address. I can understand; there are so many different options available in the marketplace, our vet tells us what to feed them, and your friends and family add their beliefs around food as well. And then there is the time factor which I hear so often. We don't take the time to prepare food for our animals in the right way. That is staggering to me, as you do take time to cook food for yourself and your family. Aren't your pets part of the family? Then let's start making time for their meals. Prepare fresh meals after you have done more research around what the best food for your pet is.

Because if we don't do this, our pets experience negative feelings, lethargy, stress, aches and pains, and sometimes depression.

One of the pets I had the privilege of connecting with was Occy; a beautiful boxer. It was a short but intense conversation, during which Occy complained of the food he was eating on a daily basis. There were a few things lacking and this needed to change so as to improve the nutritional value of what was entering his body, as well as improving his happiness.

Luckily for Occy, he had a wonderful human family around him who listened and implemented the required changes immediately. Occy experienced a positive change in his mood, health, and state of mind.

A recipe for health

The food we give our animals leaves much to be desired. Like us, some dogs love being vegetarian or vegan, and other dogs still enjoy eating meat. Unfortunately, with all the big companies out there pushing their processed food brands in the market, animals suffer a lot of discomfort and even disease, not to mention us humans being confused as to what to feed our furry family members.

More and more research[15] shows that home cooked meals and whole foods are as important for our animals as they are for us.

From the moment my dogs, Rosie and Toby, entered my life, they have eaten home cooked meals. Until a few years ago, they were also eating meat. However, this changed, as they asked to try the plant-based[12] food I am currently eating. They could see the positive changes in my body and my energy levels, so most of the time they eat the same as I do! I have noticed their bodies resonate with this diet very well, especially in their mature age.

I cook and prepare their food in advance. They dine on fresh vegetables, quinoa, barley, shredded coconut, sweet potato, and carrots, all mashed up as they are elderly and don't have many teeth left!

They love the food and the results are amazing. Toby's psoriasis has diminished, and he seems more alert. Both have more energy and crave food more, and their plates are emptied even faster than before!

Do yourself and your furry child a favour by providing healthy, home cooked, natural whole food for them, so they experience a healthier body, mind, and spirit. Besides, who doesn't want a reduced food *and* vet bill?

Being a dog-mamma, my only experience in preparing food is for dogs. My apologies to you, if you do not have a dog in your family, as the recipes below are doggy-exclusive.

Here are two of Rosie and Toby's favourite recipes. Mind you, I am not one for measurement. I just guesstimate the quantities, and I suggest you do too, tasting as you go.

This recipe makes enough for two weeks for two small dogs.

Dinner: Recipe a la Rosie and Toby

½ a pumpkin, roasted or parboiled
1 sweet potato, roasted or parboiled
4 carrots, boiled
1 cauliflower, roasted or parboiled
2 handfuls of peas
6 tbsp shredded coconut
2 tbsp flaxseed oil
½ cup apple cider vinegar

Blend the ingredients together, or mash to a fine pulp.

For variety, you may add any other greens you have in the fridge, following guidelines on certain foods which may be poisonous for dogs.

In addition, you may want to add vitamin or other nutritional supplements to their food. I suggest you perform your own research on what types to add, so that your dog (or animal companion) receives the adequate nutrients. A great starting point is talking to an 'all natural' veterinary doctor.

Snack: Baked peanut butter biscuits

2 cups rolled oats
½ cup coconut oil
4 tbsp 100% peanut butter
2 tbsp flaxseed oil
1 tsp baking powder

Add water or coconut milk and mix it all together until you have a doughy consistency.

I use some animal-shaped cutters to make the cookies, and bake them in the oven at 180°C for about 30-40 minutes.

The dogs go nuts for these!

This next recipe I received a while ago from my friend and animal naturopath, Ruth Hatten (www.ruthhatten.com). My fur-babies love this!

Veg & Bean Mash

It contains protein, antioxidants, vitamins, minerals, good fats, sulphur and anti-microbials to boot. Adding spirulina and parsley will provide a nutrient boost. For a grain-free version, leave out the oats.

1 - 2 cups of lentils or beans
½ cup rolled oats
4 - 5 cups vegetables e.g. leafy greens, zucchini, carrot, pumpkin, sweet potato, non-gmo corn
2 tbsp tahini
1 tbsp hemp seed oil
1 tsp brewers yeast (or nutritional yeast)
½ tsp kelp
1 tsp apple cider vinegar
Garlic (maximum 2 cloves per 14 kgs body weight) - optional, some dogs don't like garlic
¼ - ½ tsp spirulina - optional
Sprinkle of dried parsley - optional
1 tsp Nature's Organic Calcium

Pre-cook lentils/beans (soak overnight and cook until soft).
If using rolled oats, soak overnight.
If using pumpkin or sweet potato, lightly steam it.

Process vegetables in your food processor until they are very finely chopped. Add all other ingredients and process till it resembles a patty-like mixture.

Spoon into your canine companion's bowl and serve!

Wellbeing for both of us

Animals and humans have been living together for centuries, and it has been proven on many levels that we are of benefit to each other.

Similarly, to what I spoke about previously regarding behaviour, we also need to focus on what it means for us to live together.

Not only do animals teach us how we can best behave and live our lives, they also teach us how to look after ourselves and our health.

Animals are such sentient and loving beings, and they want us to be happy and healthy. It makes me very upset to learn that sometimes animals experience the same diseases as their human guardians, even to the point of passing away from the same condition. The reason for this, in some cases, is that the animal doesn't want us to suffer and therefore they create the dis-ease for themselves in the hope they take it away from us.

As with behaviour, it is important for us to look after our health, and how our body is performing.

Animals are very sensitive to emotions, they love healthy eating and living as well as hygiene. And that goes for us as well.

I believe we need to be extra careful with our life choices and how we care for ourselves, so that our animals are safe and healthy too.

Animals can help us with our emotional wellbeing and vice versa

We have heard this all before, as it has been proven scientifically over the years that having animals around us has enormous benefits for our mental and emotional wellbeing.

Animals all over the world are helping people with depression, grief, anxiety and disabilities. From service dogs to grief companions, the mutual support between animals and humans is well documented.[13]

They help us to have happy and loving relationships, and they know how we feel and what is needed for us. I have learned this by working with and reading about animals for so many years.

One of the articles[14] I've read talks about horses and their healing ability. The article, written by Jeremy Little from SANE Australia, explains how horses can also help us to open up if we find it difficult to talk about our experience with mental health issues. The article highlights a war veteran with PTSD and how he worked with horses to work through his trauma.

Whatever pet you have, they can help us enormously; they love us unconditionally.

On the flip side, animals too can suffer from mental health issues. They can suffer anxiety, depression and grief. I have seen this in my own dog, Toby, who sometimes has anxiety. Unfortunately, I have seen many other animals with mental health challenges who have no support from their human guardians, simply, because their human family doesn't know that their pet is suffering, and if they do, they don't know what to do about it.

In a special edition of *Time Magazine: The Animal Mind (2014)*, author Jeffrey Kluger dedicates a full chapter to mental illness in animals. He starts by explaining how he sees a dolphin in captivity swimming in circles, continuously. This is a sign of depression or even insanity due to its small enclosure.

He continues to talk about other animals showing signs of depression, such as birds plucking feathers in a cage, abused dogs retreating in terror at the sight of a human hand, or chickens on industrial farms pecking each other to death. And I can't help but wonder; why on earth would we put animals through this terror, angst and abuse? When I read this chapter, I can't help but feel extremely sad and angry at the same time. We humans put animals through this. And for what? So, we can watch them in a zoo or raise them to be consumed?

My point is, animals that live with us, even if they are treated in the best way possible, can still suffer in silence. It is up to us to *notice* the signs by *observing* the behaviour, so we can help them through their ordeal.

I'll give you a few behavioural signs you can look out for, so you can identify if your pet may be suffering from a mental illness:

- Excessive grooming
- Plucking feathers
- Poor sleep
- Loss of appetite
- Walking or swimming in circles
- Barking all day
- Biting themselves or others

These behaviours may actually be very similar to human behaviour, when experiencing mental health issues or emotional trauma. I also want to add, that the above list is not limited, but always make sure that the behaviour is not related to physical issues. For example, excessive grooming may be related to a skin condition.

We can help them by loving them unconditionally (that's a given, right?). We can also help with natural remedies, such as herbal medication, organic, home-made food, homoeopathy, Australian Bushflower Essences, music or aromatherapy oils. Oils can be dangerous for some animals, so it's important to read up on this very carefully before use.

And... these remedies are also good for us humans! Just as company is mutually beneficial, natural medicines have a lot to offer both humans and our animal friends.

What next?

Expand your knowledge and connection

There are so many layers to communicating with animals. Now, you recognise the importance of caring for ourselves as much as for the animals around us. Delving into the world of Spirit means we need to listen to our own intuition, and possibly our spirit guides, before we can effectively chat with animals.

Following the steps and guidance in this book is a wonderful place to start, and it has been a great journey and a pleasure to write and share this knowledge with you.

I feel proud, knowing that you want to make a change in the world of the animals, and a change to your own world.

I am thrilled that you are open to connecting with the animal kingdom, the spirit realms, and more importantly, helping yourself in a loving and compassionate way. I can't wait to hear some of your stories and experiences.

My wish is that you are inspired to move deeper into the world of spirit abilities with the help of the animals, for the benefit of yourself and everyone around you.

That you feel empowered to follow your heart, and enter a world of animal wisdom, where you can also be their voice.

That you feel loved, knowing that when you tap into your heart and listen to your voice, you can live a life filled with joy, love and happiness.

I'd love to bring animal communication to the world with compassion, love and joy. To help others become skilled animal communicators and voices for the animals, so we can help them, ourselves, and others around us.

When we tune into Universal language, we can help humankind and the animals, from a place of unconditional love. We can all make a difference in the world for the animals, for ourselves and live connected, compassionate lives, together in joy, freedom, harmony and love.

Thank you for taking the time to read and learn, and thank you for being part of this!

Stay Connected, with Love & Grace.

Awakening

A channelled message

Hello? Can You Hear Me?

Believe in you
the way we believe in you

Love you
the way we love you

Respect you
the way we respect you

Open your heart
the way we teach you

Shine your light bright
so others can see it

Fulfil your purpose
the way we show you

You are Light and Love
the world awakens to you

Channelled message from Azrael, the archangel of transition, Master of the Akashic records, by Bianca de Reus, 26 July 2015

Experience you, your true S.E.L.F.
and feel the love and harmony.

See the magnificent Being that
you are.

You truly are LOVE.

Acknowledgements

With gratitude, love and grace

To my family and friends

I deeply thank and am grateful for Lana, my loving wife, Soulmate, and best friend. For always believing in me, supporting and loving me unconditionally, and being by my side no matter what happens. For following along with my dreams, and walking alongside me as I fulfil my purpose. For the fun times, the challenges, the joy, love, and cocktails we share. I love you with all my heart.

Thank you to Michael, our handsome son, who is ever supportive, providing me with so much love. I have learned so much from you. I love you.

I also thank my beautiful parents, Henny and Rien, for being my mentors and teachers in this life. You are amazing Beings who have done so much, and never doubted me or my convictions. Unconditional love is what I learned from you, and I cannot thank you enough for bringing me into this world. I love you both so much.

To my brother, Rody, and his wife Christina, my soul sister, for always being there, even with the distance, loving and supporting me. For never questioning my path and knowing that I have always loved you. I love you now and always.

Last but not least, a massive thank you to those who are closest to my heart: Elma, Jappe and Fayçal, Que and Daniel, Senta, Maggie, Maria, Cor,

Ashley, Amanda, Luisa, Suzanne. For your high spirits, support, love, belief in me and teaching me. You have all kept me going and lifted me up by continuing to inspire me, providing support during challenging times, having fun, and loving me for who I am. I love you all so much.

To the wonderful, nurturing Mem, for a fun collaboration in bringing this book to life through your expert wordsmith skills, the many laughs and inspiring conversations. I have so much love and gratitude for you.

To those who helped my book become a reality. I could not have done this without your expertise, creativity, unwavering support, and love for this important part of my life: Clare and Brendan, Amanda, Barbora, Silvia, and the team at Balboa Press.

To all others around me who have nurtured, inspired and mentored me over the years, and continue to do so.

I am so blessed.

I am so grateful.

I am so thankful.

I AM.

About the author

Bianca de Reus

Bianca was born and raised in the small town of Heemskerk, in the Netherlands. She found her way to Sydney, Australia in 1996, where shortly after she was approached by a wild snake who told her what her life purpose was to be.

Bianca is an inspiring and passionate Soul Being, who loves the connections between animals and people, bringing them together with love, joy, and harmony.

She is a game changing animal communicator and soul connection mentor who works outside the norm, and takes people to a higher energy when working with animals.

She helps conscious animals lovers to create harmony and love by connecting deeply with their animal friends.

Bianca is also a warm, engaging, and inspirational speaker. She is a soul connection mentor, spiritual activist, Master Reiki and Shambala healer.

Bianca lives her life with passion and enthusiasm, learning any lessons which arise, and healing herself by stepping into her heart and reconnecting with her Soul to listen and take inspired action. This has led her to develop spiritual abilities, which empower her to share her wisdom with people around the world.

Bianca lives in Sydney, Australia with her beautiful wife, son, and two very cute and cuddly dogs.

She loves indulging in liquorice, chocolate, and whiskey, although not always together!

Bianca is a committed vegan who, in between work and travel, also enjoys photography, music, sunshine, nature, travel, cooking, and spending quality time with family and friends.

Speaking opportunities

Meet Bianca in person

Bianca is available for speaking opportunities. Her core message is: Connecting Soul Beings in Love & Harmony.

Her keynotes are highly engaging, energetic and very inspiring.

Speaking topics

Some of Bianca's speaking topics include:

- Tuning into Animal Language
- Become Familiar with Your Spirit Abilities and Connections
- Wake your S.E.L.F up!
- Creating a Co-working Space at a High Vibrational Level
- Discover Soul to Soul Connection
- Your Pet is Your Mirror

For more information and bookings, please visit www.biancadereus.com/speaker

Shine your light

Join me in Connecting Soul Beings

Receive inspiration in your inbox by signing up to my email at https://www.biancadereus.com/newsletter

Connect with other beautiful souls online at www.facebook.com/groups/connectingsoulbeings

Work with me

Learn animal communication with my full personal support and at your own pace. Check out my programs and mentoring at www.biancadereus.com

Connect with me

www.biancadereus.com
www.facebook.com/biancadereus
www.instagram.com/bianca.dereus
www.linkedin.com/in/biancadereus
www.twitter.com/biancadereus

References & glossary

1. Worldometers. (2018). *Worldometers - real time world statistics.* [online] Available at: http://www.worldometers.info [Accessed 24 July 2018].
2. Wonderopolis.org. (2018). *How Many Animals Are There in the World?* [online] Available at: https://wonderopolis.org/wonder/how-many-animals-are-there-in-the-world [Accessed 24 July 2018].
3. Conscious or consciousness:
   An awareness of the connection with Source. You who have "woken up" and work from the heart, connected to Source. Sharing your Light, and living your purpose.
4. Reiki and Shambala Healing
   Reiki means God (Rei) and Life Force Energy (ki). Reiki and Shambala multidimensional healing work on the body, mind, emotions, and spirit. This type of healing helps to release blocked energy, promote relaxation, and reduce stress. Both modalities utilise Universal Healing Energy, meaning directly from Source, and have can be effective both in person and via distance healing. For more information see: https://www.biancadereus.com/energyhealing
5. John Edward, a psychic medium able to communicate with people who have passed over.

Edward, J. (2010). *Crossing over.* New York: Sterling Pub. Co.

6. Earth Plane: "The realm of the living, as opposed to that of the spirits."
Oxford Dictionaries | English. (2018). earth plane | Definition of earth plane in English by Oxford Dictionaries. [online] Available at: https://en.oxforddictionaries.com/definition/earth_plane [Accessed 24 July 2018].

7. High Vibrational Level:
Our energy vibrates and can move between high and low levels of vitality. When we are at a low vibrational level, we feel flat, are out of balance, and everything seems heavy. Nothing seems to flow, and we seem stuck. At a high vibrational level, we are happy, positive and everything feels light and in the flow. Things happen effortlessly, as we are in alignment with our energy, and we are connected to the Source. Animals *always* live from a high vibrational level. For more information see: www.biancadereus.com/energyhealing

8. Human Guardian:
I use this term to acknowledge all the people who look after our animal friends, whether in the role of a vet, pet owner, rescuer, zoo keeper, sanctuary owner, or volunteer.

9. Fondin, M. (2018). *What Is a Chakra?* [online] The Chopra Center. Available at: https://chopra.com/articles/what-is-a-chakra [Accessed 1 August 2018].

10. Lifebeyonddeath.org. (2018). *The Spiritual Plane, the Celestial Plane and Heaven.* [online] Available at: http://www.lifebeyonddeath. org/the-spiritual-plane.html [Accessed 1 August 2018].

11. Roman, S. and Packer, D. (1989). *Opening to channel.* Tiburon, Calif.: H.J. Kramer.

12. World, G. (2018). *Good Nutrition for Healthy Vegan Dogs.* [online] Gentleworld.org. Available at: http://gentleworld.org/good-nu trition-for-healthy-vegan-dogs/ [Accessed 24 July 2018].
Angel Flinn. 2017. *4 Vegan Dog Food Recipes That Will Keep Your Puppy Healthy and Balanced.* [ONLINE] Available at: https://www. care2.com/greenliving/feeding-vegan-dogs-with-recipes.html. [Accessed 15 August 2018].

13. Wells, D.L, 2009. The Effects of Animals on Human Health and Well-Being. *Journal of Social Issues,* [Online]. 65:3, 523-543. Available at: https://spssi.onlinelibrary.wiley.com/doi/full/10.1111/j.1540-4560.2009.01612.x [Accessed 5 August 2018].
Mandy Oaklander. 2017. *Science says your pet is good for your mental health.* [ONLINE] Available at: http://time.com/4728315/science -says-pet-good-for-mental-health/. [Acces sed 5 August 2018].
Jeremy Little. 2015. *Do Pets have an impact on our mental health.* [ONLINE] Available at: https://www.sane.org/the-sane-blog/

wellbeing/friends-with-benefits-and-fur-do-pets-really-have-an-impact-on-our-mental-health. [Accessed 6 August 2018].
14. Jeremy Little. 2016. *Struggling to open up? A horse could help.* [ONLINE] Available at: https://www.sane.org/the-sane-blog/wellbeing/struggling-to-open-up-a-horse-could-help. [Accessed 6 August 2018].
15. Andrew Knight and Madelaine Leitsberger. 2016. *Vegetarian versus Meat-Based Diets for Companion Animals* [ONLINE] available at: http://www.mdpi.com/2076-2615/6/9/57/htm [Accessed 6 August 2018].